HABITATION OF HONEY

POEMS AND SONGS

NANCY PETREY

Energion Publications
Gonzalez, FL
2015

ISBN10: 1-63199-075-6
ISBN13: 978-1-63199-165-3
Library of Congress Control Number: 2015940521

Energion Publications
P. O. Box 841
Gonzalez, FL 32560

energionpubs.com
pubs@energion.com
850-525-3916

DEDICATION

In loving memory of Esther Troskey
Frank and Esther were our best friends in Columbus, Mississippi.
Their ante-bellum home is called "The Haven."

FRANK AND ESTHER
TWO RARE JEWELS

Always loving,
Caring, and there
For friends who call,
For those who need prayer.
The Kingdom is brighter,
And hearts are stronger,
For you are builders,
Encouraging longer
Than others who weary and
Lose their patience.
Esther and Frank,
Hosts of "The Haven,"
Shelter and heal
The tired and heavy-laden.
You are our friends –
We love you so much,
And we're asking God
To give you a touch!

April 12, 1995, Anniversary card

My heart is overflowing with a good theme;
I recite my composition concerning the King;
My tongue is the pen of a ready writer.
– Psalm 45:1

Table of Contents

PRAYER AND MISSION

FIRST AND SECOND COMING

Viewed from Heaven:

Acknowledgments

I am grateful for many people who helped bring me to this point of writing a book of poetry, beginning with my parents, Bertie and Nan Williams, and my high school English teacher, Evelyn Turner, who was also a family friend. They shaped my life, laying down a Christian influence and providing a good education.

I want to acknowledge my husband, Curtis Petrey, who has always been "the wind beneath my wings" in every endeavor. His wisdom and advice have been invaluable.

And tremendous thanks go to my granddaughter, Taylor Grace Petrey, a high school senior aspiring to be an architect, who has blessed me with nine drawings for this book. I appreciate her talent and am honored to facilitate her artistic debut in her first published work!

I am grateful to my publishers, Henry and Jody Neufeld, for patiently working with me on this collection of poems and being so gracious to publish my second book.

This book would not have been possible without the inspiration and guidance of the Holy Spirit and the prayers of my friends. May the Lord bless my friends bountifully for interceding for me, and may these poems glorify God and edify believers.

Introduction

I am an amateur poet. These poems came from insights and feelings that seemed to be conveyed best in a poetic format. Never having studied poetry other than what I was exposed to in school, I just wrote down my thoughts in rhyme and rhythm. It gave me a feeling of satisfaction in expressing insights from life and Scripture in this way. I was surprised when others enjoyed my poems. Several suggested I put them in a book. The Lord confirmed this and opened the door for publication.

These poems and songs are primarily inspired by Scripture and my relationship with God. The title, *Habitation of Honey*, gives a hint of the purpose I think God has for this book – preparing the way of the Lord. John the Baptist did that the first time the Messiah came to earth. He was in the wilderness, eating locusts and **wild honey**. In Scripture, the Word of God is likened to honey many times. Preparing the way of the Lord involves **eating** that honey! It is my prayer that these poems may be used in the reader's life to prepare him for the return of the Lord. The Messiah and His bride at the wedding feast is a recurring theme throughout the book.

Most of these poems give the greatest effect when read aloud. The rhythm can be enjoyed more that way. (Of course, the songs are to be sung, but I leave the music to your imagination!) Some are best read meditatively with Bible in hand. There are a few just for laughs! I have tried to arrange them somewhat topically.

I sincerely hope you are blessed by this book, but I am primarily displaying my poems for **His** approval. Paul says, "And whatever you do in word or deed, **do all in the name of the Lord Jesus**, giving thanks to God the Father through Him" (Colossians 3:17) And I do!

WORD OF GOD

HABITATION OF HONEY

(Psalm 19:7-11)

Habitation of honey, the place where sweetness dwells,
In the pages of the Bible are the words that Wisdom spells.
Words written in Hebrew, words written in Greek,
The Author changes those words into any language you speak.
If you're looking for a guide that will take you through this life,
Taste and see that He is good, He is looking for a wife!
You will need to know the history of God's people and God's plan -
The stories of heroes and villains will teach you how to stand.
The answer to every issue of life is found in this holy Book.
The Spirit of God will help you read and show you where to look.
So have a piece of the honeycomb, the habitation where honey is found.
You'll find your destiny, He will fill your cup
At the Marriage Supper of the Lamb.

January 28, 2014

Samson, Jonathan, And Ezekiel

Samson and Jonathan were strong men of the Bible –
In the heat of battle, both ate honey for revival.
Both were called of God, and they were not afraid,
But Samson lost his strength – by a maid he was betrayed.
Jonathan clung to David with a love that would not die.
He gave up a king's life to raise his friend high.
The Lord provided honey in the course of each life:
Samson used it for himself, but Jonathan sacrificed.
Samson's lust for pleasure was the goal that he pursued,
But Jonathan ate the honey, and his service was renewed.
The Word of God is sweet, but have we eaten and not obeyed?
Samson's fate was blindness; Jonathan's love was repaid.
After Jonathan's death, David kept his promise sure –
Kindness to his dear friend's son would make his name endure.
Ezekiel ate the Word of God – like honey it was sweet.
Living deep inside of him, the words he would repeat.
The captives would not hear him; rebellion filled each heart.
He spoke God's word to warn them, from sin they must depart.
I have tasted God's good Word, and by it I was warned.
I know that keeping His commands, I'll reap a great reward.

February, 14, 2014

No Condemnation!

(Based on Romans 7:19-8:4 – rapper style)

I'm no good! I'm no good!
Sins of omission! Haven't done what I should!
I seek relief in the pages of The Book –
What will God say, and where should I look?
Opening the Bible, I am sitting still.
His message describes the way that I feel.
Just like Paul, I love God's commands,
But I keep on falling – I cannot stand!
I've come to the end of the proverbial rope,
I'm reaching out to Jesus – I must have hope!
I read about Paul who felt deep despair.
He cried for deliverance, and Jesus was there!
The words leapt off of the page I read,
"There's no condemnation for you," He said!
I knew He had spoken, and I breathed a sigh.
I'll love Him forever till the day I die!
He died for me, paid for all my sin;
By His Spirit I'll walk and the victory win!
Yes, He threw out a rope, and I grabbed it fast –
His Word made the difference, and I'm no longer sad.

February 17, 2014

A MERRY HEART

(Song)

A merry heart doeth good like a medicine,
A merry heart doeth good for my soul.
I open wide my mouth, and He fills it;
I open wide my heart, He revives it.
I sing a song that I have never heard before.
A merry heart doeth good like a medicine,
A merry heart doeth good for my soul.
He satisfies my mouth with good things
So that my youth is renewed like the eagle's,
And I am lifted up on the wings of a brand new song!

He brought me up out of a horrible pit and out of the miry clay.
He set my feet upon a rock and established me in His way.
For He hath put a new song in my mouth,
even praise unto our God.
Many shall see it, and they shall fear
and shall trust in the Lord, in the Lord.

A merry heart doeth good like a medicine,
A merry heart doeth good for my soul.
He redeemeth my life from destruction.
He crowneth me with lovingkindness,
And He crowneth me with His tender mercies.
He crowneth me, He crowneth me!
He crowneth me, He crowneth me!
His love has made a merry heart!

April 27, 1989

Two Kings

(Story of King Uzziah: II Chronicles 26 and King
Nebuchadnezzar: Daniel 4)

Learn a lesson from King Uzziah, who fell because of pride.
He reigned as king for fifty-two years, disgraced when he died.
As King of Judah he followed the Lord
and rose to the pinnacle of power,
But thinking he could do as he pleased, he fell in a single hour.
He went to the temple with his censer in hand,
planning to be a priest,
But the priests came in and confronted his sin
and told him he must cease.
His face grew red, and his anger flared,
and the priests took one step back,
But they gasped when they saw how judgment had come:
now the king had a breaking out!
On his forehead a spot of leprosy grew, and this was a fatal sign
That the king could no longer rule the land,
in isolation he would abide.

No matter how mighty you have become,
please let me bend your ear:
"Do justice, love mercy, walk humbly before your God
with reverent fear."

Nebuchadnezzar is another king, a ruthless one at that.
He never followed the God of Israel while on his throne he sat.
But God had mercy and revealed to him
the "Fourth Man" in the fire -
The Son of God for the three young men
had stopped their fate so dire.
Nebuchadnezzar proclaimed to his subjects

that they must worship this God,
For no other god could deliver like this,
but the king had pride and forgot!
He had a bad dream of his future doom,
and Daniel the prophet was summoned,
Who gave the meaning and warned the king
that he must repent or be humbled.
The pride of the king got the best of him,
and he bragged on the Babylon he built.
So his kingdom was taken away from him;
with the beasts of the field he dwelt.
His hair grew long, and his nails were claws;
he ate grass, and he went insane.
Seven years later he looked to heaven
and began to honor God's holy name.
Nebuchadnezzar was restored to his kingdom
– he had learned his lesson well,
That God Most High was Ruler forever
– God's works of truth he would tell.

God is able to raise the humble,
but the proud He will put down.
His ways are just, but His mercy endures.
At His feet we will lay our crowns!

January 28, 2014

Neither Jew nor Arab

Caring and correctness weighing on my heart;
Jesus did the unexpected – they should never part.
Canaanite woman falling at His feet.
Throwing her crumbs was all she did beseech.
But Jesus saw her heart, and it pained Him so.
She wasn't of the chosen race – He couldn't let her go.
He drew the faith out of her and gave her a reward:
Correctness was satisfied – choosing, He was Lord!
Love was flowing out of Him – He grafted her in.
Her status was assured that day, paid in full her sin.
Neither Jew nor Arab, a Canaanite was friend.
Caring makes them **"one new man"** – oneness is the end.*

November 18, 2014

---

* REFLECTIONS: Story of Jesus and the Canaanite woman, a Gentile (Matthew 15:21-28). She was a "wild branch" grafted into the Jewish olive tree (Romans 11:17, 24). "One new man" comes from Jesus' sacrifice, breaking down the barrier between Jew and Gentile (Ephesians 2:14-16). Arabs are Gentiles. "There is neither Jew nor Greek [Gentile] … slave nor free … male nor female; for you are all one in Christ Jesus. And if you are Christ's, then you are Abraham's seed, and heirs according to the promise" (Galalatians 3:28-29).

GOD BEHIND THE SCENES

Esther is a queen of great renown;
God made sure she got the crown.
The Jews would die without her help.
One night the king had not slept;
Books were brought, and he saw recorded
The deed of Mordecai not rewarded.
Haman came into the court that day,
Just as the king had something to say.
He ordered Haman to use his advice
To honor the man who had saved the king's life.
So Haman paraded this man through the street,
Dressed like the king. "Give honor!" he'd repeat.

Haman had built a gallows to end
The life of the Jew who would not bend,
But now his wife and wise men said,
"If Mordecai's Jewish, you're as good as dead!"
The gallows so high, not built for naught,
Were waiting till days of justice were sought;
For Mordecai's foe and his ten sons instead
Were hung by the neck until they were dead!

The plot that determined the death of the Jews,
The date that was chosen only brought good news!
Because Queen Esther went into the king,
He held out his scepter, and made her heart sing.
She did not keep silent, though her life was at risk;
She had come to the kingdom for such a time as this!
And even though God is not mentioned by name,
He's there in the Book of Esther the same.
Behind the scenes He's directing the action –

He uses the weeping, the prayers, and the fasting,
Infuses His heroine with courage driven,
Inspires the scheme of the banquets given.

The Jews would not lay a hand on the plunder
Of the wicked attacking when they had gone under.
Remembering Abram and what he replied
To the King of Sodom, his riches denied.
The descendants of Agag, Haman and sons,
All meet their deaths, and the victory's won.
It was God who controlled the throw of the "pur."
Purim would be celebrated each year for sure!
Mordecai reigned as number two man
Beside King Ahasuerus over the Persian land.
Queen Esther, the queen who saved her people,
The Jews, God's chosen, won out over evil!

April 30, 2015

CREATION

You Stir the Depths of My Soul

Viewing the beauties of creation I marvel,
Letting You stir the depths of my soul,
Thrilling to majesty, grandeur, and splendor,
Longing to stay in Your waters that roll,
Stretching to see the Creator revealed,
Wishing to give You my all, now I yield!

My Silent Savior is not of this world –
Above it He spoke, and planets were hurled.
If only His creatures would consider the Source
Of beauty and truth, they would never divorce
Creator from creation, the reflection of God –
Infinite, awesome, yet with sandals shod!

May 9, 1998

You Are A Masterpiece

Have you ever wanted to be someone else?
Is it hard for you to accept yourself?
If so, your focus is too much on you -
To God above, the glory is due.
"It is He who has made us and not we ourselves,"
From the tops of our heads to the little toenails.
Our personalities, yes, they were formed by Him, too.
I say, "Vive la différence!" I appreciate you!
Jealousy and envy should have no place -
But admiration should cover your face.
Maybe your body is handicapped,
Causing you grief, your energies sapped.
But God has never made a mistake -
The devil wants your faith to shake.
Your God is working in ways unseen
To make you shine and on Him lean.
Just look around, and you will see
His humor, beauty, and va-ri-e-ty!
Take the time to med-i-tate,
Observe and enjoy what He did create.
Relax and know you're a masterpiece,
And so is the one who's disturbing your peace!
Go easy on taking yourself apart -
Would you like the job of making a heart?
God in His wisdom needed someone like you
To round out creation of every color and hue.
Joy will come when you give Him your praise,
Appreciate your brother, and walk in God's ways.
He's making you look like His own perfect Son,
His glorious Beloved. Stay still till He's done!

March 14, 2003

DIVINE ARTIST

Seven billion people breathe the air on planet earth.
God has numbered every hair on every head – what worth!
He has made the grains of sand and knows their number, too.
And even every snowflake falling can't escape His view.
Each grain and flake are singular; no two are just alike!
My mind is boggled that He deems them precious in His sight.
Just look at all around you and appreciate His skill,
The grandeur of a mountain or a humble ant hill.
The marvel of your fingers, and the thousand things they do,
Your muscles, blood and bones are moving at the brain's cue.
Your heart just goes on beating without effort on your part,
And God, "Divine Conductor," makes it stop and makes it start.

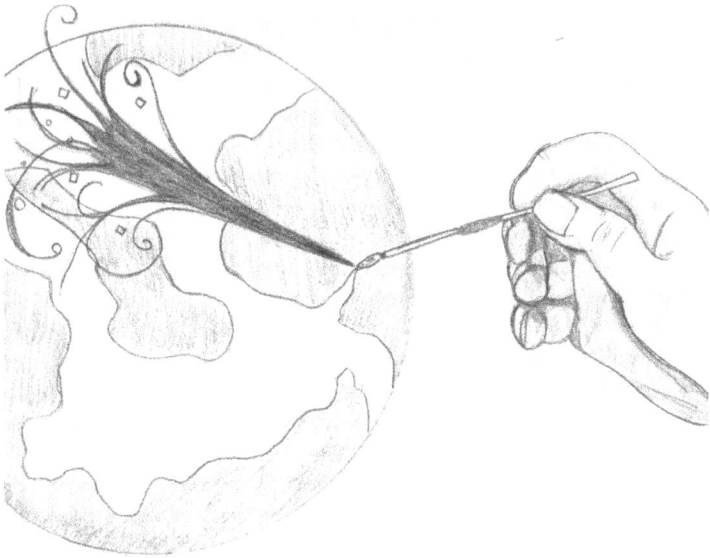

Animals, plants and rocks, sparkling bodies in the sky
Perform the things assigned to them and will until they die.

He counts and names the stars and makes the constellations* speak
The story of redemption in a pattern quite unique!
But greater still He values all the humans in His image,
Not only those who live today, but past and future lineage.
This multitude of human souls are those He died to save.
Our Jesus gave His sinless life to keep us from the grave!
God knows the ones who love His Son – they'll gather round His throne,
But man can't number this great crowd – their voices rise as one
In praise to Him who bore their sin, their every evil deed
Their thoughts, their words, their curses hurled! He met their deepest need.
His care for things inanimate expressed in myriad ways
Is proof His greatest work of art will never leave His gaze.
No fingerprint the same and not a heart is fashioned twice,
No person is designed by random choice, like throwing dice.
Our God ordained a plan for you, for every breathing soul.
His tapestry eternal will be something to behold.
So please be still in His hands, the Artist will remake
The subjects of His kingdom come, He's working to create.
It has not entered the minds of men the wonders He's prepared
In heaven with His loved ones, where His glory they will share.
So worship Him, the King of kings, Who gives you a new name.
One day you'll sing a new song to the King and with Him reign!

January 28, 2014

---

* http://www.prophecyinthenews.com/lesson-13-the-gospel-in-the-stars-part-1/

MAGNIFICENT BUT STUPID!

(Job 39:13-18)

God made it so we can learn from the animals –
Traits they have are worse than the cannibals!
Consider an ostrich with feet so swift –
She lays her eggs where a lion could sniff,
The top of the ground in broad daylight,
And off she walks without a care in sight!
When danger comes, she puts her head
Into a hole in the ground to remove her dread.
As long as she can't see it approach,
The lion's not there, and he won't encroach!
So what can we learn from this stupid bird?
What lesson is there that we haven't heard?
It's plain to see she doesn't care
If her young live or die, so she leaves them there
To fend for themselves while she takes flight –
Her speed magnificent, she's soon out of sight!
God didn't give her the wisdom of some,
But she still has value even if she's dumb!
And if you aren't as smart as a whip,
Don't think your Creator doesn't "give a flip!"
The thing He gave you is to make Him shine,
So enjoy His gift and quit your cryin'!

April 14, 2014

WRITING

POET TO POET

Expressing myself line upon line
Is something I choose to do with my time.
I marvel to see a poem take shape
As thoughts assemble in folds like a drape.
Containing my phrases within a rhyme scheme
Gives boundaries and order for stating my theme.
You wonder if what I produce is by chance,
But God gives the thought and lets me enhance.
I want to draw out the things deep inside
And cause one to ponder and look for the Guide,
Who shows us the Truth for which poets quest
And brings us the Word wherein we find rest.
So what do I say, and what do I write?
A poem with rhythm and rhyme to give light.
I just want to say in a way you can't miss
That there is an answer to life, and it's this:
Jesus is Alpha, and all we create
Must needs come from Him, the Creator great!
Jesus is Omega and all in between.
If you would have Life and see the unseen,
Look at His life, hear His own word,
Open your heart, and let Him be heard.
His beauty will startle your deepest senses,
His love will cause you to mend all your fences.
Your poems will flow from a spirit renewed
With purpose and ardor and power endued.
You'll settle the question every man asks,
Who am I beneath all these masks?

You'll know that you're His, made for His praise,
And all that you write will tell of His ways.
So poet to poet, here is my rhyme –
Writing is fun; it redeems the time.

SING-SONG DITTY

(Rapper style)

A poetic soul, I never thought I'd be.
A mystic dreamer? Heavens, that's not me!
But God flowed rhymes, and I filled with glee.
A sing-song ditty, so silly, but free!
God made rhythm by His good grace,
To keep all of life on this planet in place.
Hearts beat steady, whether fast or slow,
Our Maker conducts His creatures here below.
A season will come, and a season will go.
Rotation is sure, and it makes a show!
The rhythm and rhyme of a graceful dance
Is surely from heaven, you can tell at a glance.
The birds' migration – same time each year –
Has a way of filling your heart with cheer.
You see, all of nature just has to respond
When Yahveh, the Conductor, raises His baton.
So I will join in with my sing-song ditty
With praise in my heart. Please say, "Quite pretty!"

January 23, 2014

AMANUENSIS – SECRETARY

(Author of *Jewish Roots Journey, Memoirs of a Mizpah*, ©2012)

Scribes of Scripture often wrote
Lines of poetry that they spoke.
God can move the hand of man
To take His message across the land.

As the moon shines in the night,
It reflects the sunshine bright.
It has no light to call its own
But stands in place to make Him known!

I marvel at the words I've penned,
Inspired by Him, so He can send
To places I may never see,
To open hearts with this frail key.

An earthen vessel, I cannot boast.
I only want to be His host,
To let His Spirit move and fill
And give to me His writing skill.

Amanuensis – secretary,[*]
That I am, just ordinary.
A watchman, a lookout, on the walls,
Sounding the alarm before the night falls.

---

[*] Tertius was Paul's secretary or amanuensis.

I write and I pray, giving Him no rest.
The peace of Jerusalem is my request,
Till the Jews are ready to welcome their King,
The King of the Jews – may YESHUA'S NAME RING!*

July 13, 2012

יֵשׁוּעַ

---

* *Yeshua* means "God is salvation."

RELATIONSHIP

Sit Quietly

As the butterfly flitting from flower to flower,
You've tasted the nectar in this world's hour.
Your wings have shimmered with light from above,
But I would tuck you under my wing, little dove.
You'll never want to fly away,
Nestled by Me, you'll want to stay.
You will hear my heart, if you lie very still,
And you'll have my power working in your will.
Come away, little one, have a season of rest.
Fulfillment you'll find in your life-long quest.
I'm calling you now – can you hear my voice?
I've given you freedom to make that choice.
There are seasons in life, and you've run the race,
But nothing is better than seeing My face.
Sit quietly now, look up at My smile.
I've been gazing at you a long, long while.

April 1996

SIT AT MY FEET

(Luke 10: 38-42)

"Martha, Martha, sit at My feet,
Learn from your Rabbi, Who is lowly and meek.
Look for a break from the tasks of the day.
An oasis is waiting; I'll show you the way.
Tithe your time, and don't rob from Me.
Take it right off the top of your day, and you'll see:
The jewels I've scattered in the pages of The Book
Are there for the taking – I'll show you where to look.
The treasures of life aren't held in your hand,
They're stored in your heart, so you'll understand -
The natural things are merely reflections
Of the spiritual things - you'll see the connection.
So come to My feet in the early morn
And also the times when you're weary and worn.
I'll watch the house and look over the sheep.
You take your rest, and sit at My feet."

January 21, 2014

JUST REST, BE BLESSED

Don't be in a rush, just rest.
Enjoy your Sabbath in your nest.
Worldly distractions crowd at your door.
Don't open to them, although they roar.
Focus on God - in Him delight.
He designed your body to need His might.
Working so hard will destroy your peace,
But resting in Him, your faith will increase.
Shabbat shalom! The seventh day is here.
Yeshua is smiling - His coming is near.
As it was in the garden in the cool of the day,
We'll be walking with Him in a brand new way.
He'll set up His kingdom in the 7,000th year
In New Jerusalem, our city so dear.
Each Sabbath we rest in our current life
Is a picture of heaven where there'll be no strife.
So obey the commandment God made out of love:
Remember the Sabbath — be blessed from above.[†]

---

* Peaceful Sabbath (greeting in Israel)

† (Genesis 2:3; Exodus 20:8-11; Isaiah 58:13-14; Mark 2:27-28; Hebrews 4:1-11; Revelation 21: 2-3)

Set Free!

"Why so downcast, oh my soul?"
David cried, but I know who stole –
Satan, devil, adversary, snake!
He did his best my faith to shake.
With heavy heart and clouded eyes
I tried unknotting the knots with sighs.
No way out, the pieces wouldn't fit,
And Worry was king, on the throne did sit.
Extending his scepter and ruling with fear,
He distorted the truth till nothing was clear.
Then hope started rising from the Spirit in me.
When the truth was uncovered, my mind was set free!
The source of the torture was finally exposed
By the One who loves me and gives sweet repose.

August 6, 2012

I Am that I Am

He is Hope for the hopeless.
He is Healer for the Hurting.
He is Helper for the helpless.
He is Lover for the loser.
He is Lord for the least.
He is Savior for the sinner.
He is Shepherd for the seeker.
He is Counselor for the confused.
He is Wonderful for the wanderer.
And He is yearning for you.

August, 2002

My Trouble Shooter

Jesus is my trouble shooter – I am not alone.
Jesus gives me hope again, when things keep going wrong.
When I lie awake at night, reviewing all my woes,
I need to cast my care on Him – He'll take my heavy load.
So praising Him and thanking Him is what I need to do
Instead of whining and complaining, staying in a stew.
Yes, Jesus shoots my troubles, and He takes me up on high
To see the beauty of my life and to know I'll never die.

June, 2, 2003

HIS MIGHTY WINGS

The wings of my God are mighty over me,
Dwelling in His shadow, as peaceful as can be.
Covered by His feathers, in His tabernacle safe,
I have taken refuge in His awesome, secret place!
Yeshua is my Savior, and like a mother hen,
His wings provide shelter till the very end.
He's also like an eagle with pinions very strong,
Snatching me from dangers of an evil, rioting throng!

The Father has adopted me, His eaglet in the nest –
I cry unto Him, "Abba,"* and I rest upon His breast.
He tells me of my heritage and instructs me in His Word,
From Abraham to Moses, oh what miracles I've heard!
"I bore you on eagles' wings and brought you to Myself.
In the mighty Exodus, you saw the judgments dealt.
Your enemies were conquered, and you escaped death.
I uttered Ten Commandments with My thundering breath.
I saved you by the blood of the Passover Lamb.
Then I split the Red Sea, I Am the Great I Am!
I made a covenant with you, My very special treasure,
You are My chosen people, My greatest source of pleasure.

"My eaglet, I did keep you as the apple of My eye
And hovered closely o'er you until you learned to fly.

---

*   Romans 8:15

I stirred up your nest and took away your ease -
I allowed many hardships to bring you to your knees.
But just as you were falling, I would spread out My wings,
And I would take you high above, and you would shout and sing!"

God's dealings with the Israelites and with their Holy City
Are written in Scripture, and some are not so pretty.
But learning from mistakes, God means to give us hope –
We can rise on wings like eagles, not in the darkness grope.
We will run and not be weary; we will walk and never faint.
When the day of wrath has come, it won't come upon His saint.

The Sun of Righteousness shall rise with healing in His wings.
The wicked on a burning earth will hear our voices sing
"As the Lord of Hosts fights for Mount Zion and its hill,
Like birds flying about, passing over" – what a thrill!
So when the storm is raging, and you've nowhere else to turn,
Seek the wings of the Eagle, from His lessons you will learn.
Whether flying high above the storm or resting in His shade,
You can have your youth renewed; from destruction you are saved.

Yeshua's calling out to you to wrap in His tallit,
His arms are stretching forth – under His wings you are complete.*
So learn your Jewish roots, a Jewish wedding is the goal.
Messiah's waiting for you in the chuppah to enfold.
To wrap in His tallit, under the canopy of another,
You'll enjoy the Wedding Feast in the arms of a Jewish lover!

July 5, 2014

---

* "The hem of His garment" that the woman with the issue of blood touched
in Matthew 9:20 indicates the tassels or "wings" on the four corners of His prayer
shawl or tallit. See a tallit pictured on page 76.

Message from a Sparrow

A lone, tiny sparrow at the Father's command
Came bearing a message held in my husband's hand.
The sparrow was silent, but his presence did say
That the song I was singing was under God's sway.
How else could my husband hold a bird in his hand,
When birds always scatter if near them you stand?
Be aware of His presence, He's watching you, too.
He's taking delight in the things that you do.
You can't count His thoughts, they're like grains of sand,
But His words I did sing at my piano grand.
My husband uttered a prophecy true -
"His eye is on the sparrow, and He's watching you!"
The sparrow was finished, he had acted on cue.
My husband released him, and away he flew!
The air was settled, my confidence regained,
I would proceed with the concert to honor His name.
The bird had assured me the Lord was well-pleased.
He had provided this piano for His praises indeed!*

January 23, 2014

---

* Nancy's amazing testimony in *Jewish Roots Journey, Memoirs of a Mizpah*,
Nancy Petrey (Energion Publications: Gonzalez, FL) p. 81-82

Feeling His Affirmation

Faith is a fact, not a feeling,
But I want my senses reeling!
I want to see and touch
The Master's face so much.
To feel His arms around me,
To feel I'm sitting on His knee!
This is my life-long quest,
To be leaning upon His breast,
A quest over all supreme
And not just a fleeting dream.

The children were welcome to come,
And He blessed them every one.
I can picture their play in the grass,
Their laughing and running so fast.
Jesus would make them feel right,
His loving acceptance so bright.
He drove all their fears away,
As He danced in their circle of play.
I dare say He danced with me, too.
It happened just out of the blue!

Approaching me with a smile,
This man asked to dance a while.
Saying, "Jesus will dance with you,"
He took my hand, and we flew!
Seeing the thoughts in my head,
Jesus sent this man in His stead!
It is quite an amazing thing
And it makes your spirit sing.

He knows your anxious heart,
His arrow of love hits its mark.
He catches you by surprise,
His ways you will never surmise.
But He knows just how to affirm
And meet you right where you yearn.
In His own time and way
Things turn out right – don't dismay.

February 3, 2014

LINGER

(in the Upper Room of the Jerusalem Prayer Center)

Child, I want you to linger here.
You feel My presence, you know I'm near –
The quietness, the stillness, I'm soothing your soul.
Your fears are protesting, but I'm in control.
What better way to spend your time?
Than reading My words – the Truth is sublime.
Drink deep of My Spirit and then go forth.
I love you, my child, you are of great worth.
Just sprinkle the diamonds you have found in here,
And pour forth the fragrance, My beauty so clear.
Others will know Me, for you took the time
To linger and bask in My presence divine.*

October 1, 2012

---

* Visiting the Upper Room in the Jerusalem Prayer Center on my seventh trip to Israel was one of the greatest spiritual experiences of my life. It was an interactive prayer room with stations around the room where you could sit on a pillow or chair and meditate on Scriptures written in English, Hebrew, and Arabic on beautiful wall banners, soaking in the manifest presence of God. Journals were available to record your thoughts and prayers. At one station you could examine your heart and write out a prayer asking forgiveness, then put the slip of paper in a vat of liquid. It looked like water, but when stirred, the paper would disappear! Stations with media presentations of mission needs and wall maps of the world and Israel, marked with the Jewish and Arab churches, were places for intercessory prayer. You could write names of loved ones or people groups needing salvation with colored markers on rocks placed in a basket. A large table was filled with sketch books for creative drawing or writing prayers and poems. We stayed a long time in that room, and I did not want to leave. I sat down and wrote this poem, expressing what I was feeling in that holy place.

Take Time to Smell the Roses

(Song written for a kindergarten class program I taught.)

Take time to smell the roses, Mom. Take time to hold my hand.
Take time to hear my problems and to say you understand.
Take time to play a game with me, to throw and catch a ball.
Take time to say you love me and to see I'm growing tall.

(Chorus):
Take time to smell the roses when they're blooming.
Take time to smell the roses when they're there.
Take time to smell the roses when they're blooming,
For I'm your rose – please show me that you care.

Take time to smell the roses, Dad. Take time to talk with me.
Take time to let me hug your neck. Take time to really see
That I am growing up so fast, I need your help each day
To guide me in the things I do at school and church and play.

(Chorus): Take time to smell the roses when they're blooming.
Take time to smell the roses when they're there.
Take time to smell the roses when they're blooming,
For I'm your rose – please show me that you care.

July 27, 1989

PRAYER AND MISSION

INTERCESSION

I really love lifting Your children to You,
To help with what they are going through.
They shouldn't have to bear burdens alone,
When they've got a friend who can go to Your throne.
I may not make a fine casserole,
But You will listen to a prayer that is bold,
A plea I can make for my friend or my kin,
And leave it to Jesus – His mercy won't end.
He said we should pray and simply believe
The Father will answer, and we will receive.
God's ways are lofty, His thoughts high indeed.
He says, "Don't grow weary. I want you to plead.
I'm teaching you reigning – this world your domain.
Your prayers are important; they're not prayed in vain.
Don't think what is meant will come without you,
That My kingdom on earth will come right on cue.
Consider that Moses did stay My hand,
And Daniel by fasting did understand
The times of his people, the angel foretold.
Their prayers made the difference – My plan could unfold!"
So stand in the gap, whether good times or bad,
And pray for your loved ones, whether happy or sad.
Take out your Bible, find the things on God's heart.
Your prayers for Jerusalem will make a good start.
We're not to keep silent in our place on the wall –
What concerns His city is what concerns us all.
For one day our King will return there in power –
The prayers of the saints have prepared for this hour.
Our intercession is incense before the golden altar,
So, child, keep on praying, and don't you falter.

The King is coming, He's bringing His bride;
She'll be clothed in white and will sit by His side.
Her training for reigning, her prayers in one accord
Bring the kingdom of heaven. **The King** is her reward!

January 22, 2014

Seek His Face

(About the increasing persecution of Christians
in the United States)

Seek His face, not His hand;
He is looking at our land.
Tears are streaming down His face,
As His people are disgraced.
When they speak the truth in love,
They receive a brutal shove!
Feel the heart of God our Father;
Don't say, "Why now should I bother?"
Jesus went down on His knees;
For the city were His pleas.
How He wept, His heart was sore.
"You will see My face no more,
Till you bless Me, turn from sin,
Then I'll come to you again."
Seek His face and not His hand;
Feel His heart and understand,
It is not His heart's desire
To bring brimstone, smoke, and fire!
"America! Do you want to die?
Why do you believe the lie
Your success has come from man?
It has come by My own hand!"
We who know we're blessed by Him
Should not seek our every whim.
We should seek His face, not hand,
Praying God will heal our land.

December 19, 2013

Tears upon the Altar

The benediction spoken, people hurried for the door,
But passing by the altar I saw tears from a heart so sore.
I stopped and gazed at shining tears – to me they seemed to say
That Jesus cleansed away the hurt and touched the feet of clay.

Tears upon the altar are a symbol of this place,
Where burdens can be lifted by a mighty God of grace.
Don't wait when He is reaching out to help you on your way.
Come to the altar and kneel down – He'll hear you when you pray.
Some people try to hide their pain and never let it show,
But Jesus said, "Come to Me, My peace you'll surely know."
You'll find that there are others who can help you bear your load.
So take it to the altar – He has paid the debt you owed!

(ca. 1982, at Faith United Methodist Church in Southaven, Mississippi)

A Musician's Prayer

Let my heart flow with love for my Savior above,
Who stepped down from glory as gentle as a dove.
Let my works always be for You and not for me,
To give You greatest glory, not so I can charge a fee.

Let my singing touch Your heart,
Let my playing make it rain.
For your pleasure and Your purpose
Let it heal the people's pain.
For Your gift of music, thank you –
Makes us laugh and makes us cry,
Makes us dance, inspires our worship
As we offer it on High.
Help me paint the clearest picture
Of Your beauty and Your truth.

Your truth is what grabs us, Your beauty makes us sigh,
But Your loving arms around us is what holds us till we die.
Let me sing, let me play, let me live for You alone,
Let me hear a loud applause coming from Your holy throne!

January 21, 2014

It's Time to Move!

(Song)

There burns in my soul a song to sing,
A message to shout so the church will move out.
I've glimpsed the glory prepared for us –
Take the land, there's healing in your hand!

(Chorus): It's time, it's time to move, it's time, it's time to move,
It's time, it's time, it's time to move,
It's time to move out for God!

Let your fears just drop to the floor,
Take your faith, and sweep them out the door!
It's time, it's time, it's time to move,
it's time to move out for God!

Our songs are the weapons we wield,
And our faith, we hold up as a shield.
It's time, it's time, it's time to move,
it's time to move out for God!

Our Captain of the hosts says, "Go!"
We follow, and we trample the foe!
It's time, it's time, it's time to move,
it's time to move out for God!

We'll go to set the captives free,
In His name we'll make the enemy flee!
It's time, it's time, it's time to move,it's time to move out for God!

(Chorus): It's time, it's time to move, it's time, it's time to move,
It's time, it's time, it's time to move,
It's time to move out for God!

May 9, 1987

LIGHT BREAKS THROUGH DARKNESS

What is rhyme, and what is verse?
Expresses the heart at length or terse.
Looking deep within my soul
To find a word one can behold,
Evoking warmth in truth and splendor
To reach someone very tender.
The Poet uses me, a vessel,
So that in His arms you'll nestle.
Taste the honey, drink the wine,
Eat the bread, and be a sign.
You're His bride, wear His ring,
Preach His message, pray, and sing.
Terror spreads, heads are falling!
Seek His quietness, know your calling.
Cities burn, hate increases,
Do not wait until war ceases.
Lift the banner of His name,
Love the enemy, despise the shame.
Till light breaks through the darkness deep,
Win the lost with Love, don't sleep!*

April 29, 2015

---

* Reflecting on a Christian's response to riots in America and persecution of Christians in the Middle East.

MESSENGER

(Chorus 1)
I am a messenger girl for Messiah Yeshua,
His name is Jesus!
I'll take His word to the world, but first to the Jew,
And where His Spirit leads me.
I will be bold, and I will have no fear.
His Spirit is in me, and His call is clear.
I'll spread His love, and I'll sing and praise His name.

Yes, the world needs to hear about Jesus,
He's the cure for their darkness and sin.
The harvest is ripe – won't you lift up your eyes?
Tell them Jesus has forgiveness for them!
The world may be your next door neighbor
Or even your next of kin.
Just heed the Master's voice, and make your choice,
You will follow Him till the end!

(Chorus 2):
We are the messengers sent by Messiah Yeshua,
His name is Jesus!
We'll take His word to the world, but first to the Jew,
And where His Spirit leads us.
We will be bold, and we will have no fear.
His Spirit is in us, and His call is clear.
We'll spread His love, and we'll sing and praise His name.

There are people who will listen to you
By what you say and by what you do,
But they may have a different language, live across the earth,
But when you speak, they will have a new birth!

We are the messengers sent by Messiah Yeshua,
His name is Jesus!
We'll take His word to the world, but first to the Jew,
And where His Spirit leads us.
We will be bold, and we will have no fear.
His Spirit is in us, and His call is clear.
We'll spread His love, and we'll sing,
We'll spread His love, and we'll pray,
We'll spread His love, and we'll preach
And praise His name!*

June 4, 1995

---

* Song written for a mission team going out from Columbus, Mississippi to Israel, which I later applied to myself as a "Mizpah," meaning watchman and witness, for Israel.

Prophecy in a Greeting Card

(Confirming a trip to Israel on September-October 2012)

I have a friend who blessed me with an uplifting word.
She used a butterfly, and from God I think I heard –
"Love is like a butterfly" – words upon a card.
She didn't know I soon would be going very far –
"It goes where it pleases and pleases where it goes."
The card showed a sunrise at the end of a road.
A butterfly was floating right beside the pretty words.
She sent two more besides, that flew out just like birds!
Inside my friend had written, and the words blessed my heart.
She ended with a prophecy that surely hit the mark.
For I had struggled anxiously and prayed that I would know
If God had truly beckoned me and said for me to go.
"Rest in His Precious Arms," she wrote,
"For He has greater plans
For you than you could ask or imagine!" I WAS in His hands!
Yes, God can speak His word, using even you and me,
So let Him have your hands and voice –
your words may be a key –
A prophecy to help someone to know that they are loved
And valued so that God would send His message from above.

August 6, 2012

INTO THE BATTLE

In Congress and Cathedral the prayers of the Muslims,
Invoking their god, are pushing my buttons!
Goliath is taunting and testing our mettle –
Oh, but we yawn, on the sofa we settle.
Let someone else go out with a sword,
I'll do my routine, I had rather be bored.
Muslims are gaining new ground inch by inch,
We won't look that way – we don't have a wrench.
We know we can't fix it – we'll say a quick prayer,
While Satan is dragging more souls to his lair.
A bold and brave word the blond woman uttered,
Stood up for Jesus, and the demons they shuddered.
All it will take to make the giant fall
Is a stone in a sling and a faith nine feet tall!
So stand at your watch, and listen for orders,
Take into the battle God's Word, and don't loiter.
Lift up your voice in the square of the city,
And when you're on trial, He gives words that are fitting!
So be like a Deborah, a David, or Gideon –
Exalting Jesus, with His Spirit, not quitting!*

---

* Written November 17, 2014, after hearing about an Islamic Imam opening
Congress with prayer to Allah on November 13, 2014. The Imam was praised by
Speaker Boehner and no protest was registered. The second incident of Muslim
prayers being offered was the next day in the National Cathedral in Washington,
D.C. with worshipers on prayer mats. This did elicit one protest from a Christian woman, a blonde, who was promptly escorted out of the Cathedral!

THE MIDNIGHT RIDE

The midnight ride of Paul Revere –
He warned the people that danger was near.
The British were coming – they meant great harm.
He had to ride and spread the alarm.
Prophets today have a mission like his,
To tell the truth while calming their fears.
The world is burning, but God's not dead.
He provides a shelter and takes away dread.
"Look to Me, all ye ends of the earth;
I will save you. Each soul has great worth.
But if you choose to go your own way,
Your soul will perish! Why don't you pray?"
The British are coming, the clock strikes twelve –
Go into the Ark – in Jesus to dwell.

November 14, 2014

FIRST AND SECOND COMING

SHEPHERDS AND KINGS

(Prophetic poem. Story of the shepherds – Luke 2:8-20.
Story of the kings – Matthew 2:1-12.)

SHEPHERDS with the sheep,
That night they couldn't sleep.
'Twas stirring in the air,
And they had the weight of care.
But look! The sky above
Shone bright, and they felt love.
Frightened by the sight,
Yet strengthened by the Light.
Angels! Myriads! Singing!
Across the heavens ringing!
They spoke of just a Baby
Who **would** be King, not **maybe**.
The Messiah God appointed
For all men – His Anointed.

The shepherds left their sheep and ran.
They had to see this Baby – grand!
They found Him as the angel said,
Wrapped in cloths in a manger bed.
Why did God choose shepherds low
To visit first and see the glow?
To gaze at Diety's face unveiled,
Then tell the world what they beheld?
God chose shepherds when first He came
To show us all **He** was the **same**.
To poor He gave the tidings **first** -
Good will to man and peace on earth.
God and shepherds, you and me -
His first coming. Can't you see?

KINGS from afar, following a star,
Coming to the place, by His blessed grace.
The star shone bright at night,
Giving them light.
Gentiles, rich and wise,
Looking for the Prize.
No angel had to tell them,
No circumstance compel them.
Traveling through the countryside,
Keeping their gaze on the skies.
Could this show the **Second** Advent?
Is this a picture of God's intent?

Two years since the Baby came
Could mean two thousand, just the same.
The **sign** of His coming, a **second** star?
Look up and hope, the time is not far.
Shepherds and kings speak of these things:
A Lamb for the shepherds,
A Lion for the kings.
Poor and rich, Jesus comes to all –
Lowly, yet kingly – hear the midnight call.
When things get dark, and the journey's long,
Just look for the star over a world gone wrong.
Jesus will come like a thief in the night,
The Bright Morning Star bursting forth in the light!
The Good Shepherd laid down His life for the sheep,
But the King comes to rule and His promises keep.

November 29, 1999

A Happy Day!

(Dedicated to those who have sad moments at Christmas,
remembering loved ones they have lost.)

Jesus stepped down from His glorious throne
To be one of us, a human, flesh and bone.
He had to depend on His mother alone
To feed Him and clean Him and give Him a home.
He limited Himself to a frail human frame,
His own power gone, only power in God's name.
This pattern He gave to the ones who believe:
They can act by the Spirit and do miracles indeed!
Imagine that Jesus, who was born to reign,
Would be crowned with thorns, crucified with pain.
So remember at Christmas, by His cradle we stand,
That suffering and sorrow
would be allowed by God's hand.

Over the cradle fell the shadow of the cross,
But He rose from the dead and saved the lost.
So don't give up when your life goes sour,
For this could be your finest hour.
Suffering and sorrow may dog your steps,
But rejoice and be glad! It's not over yet!
One day the tears will be wiped away
When the Bright, Morning Star
Brings a **happy** day!

December 23, 2013

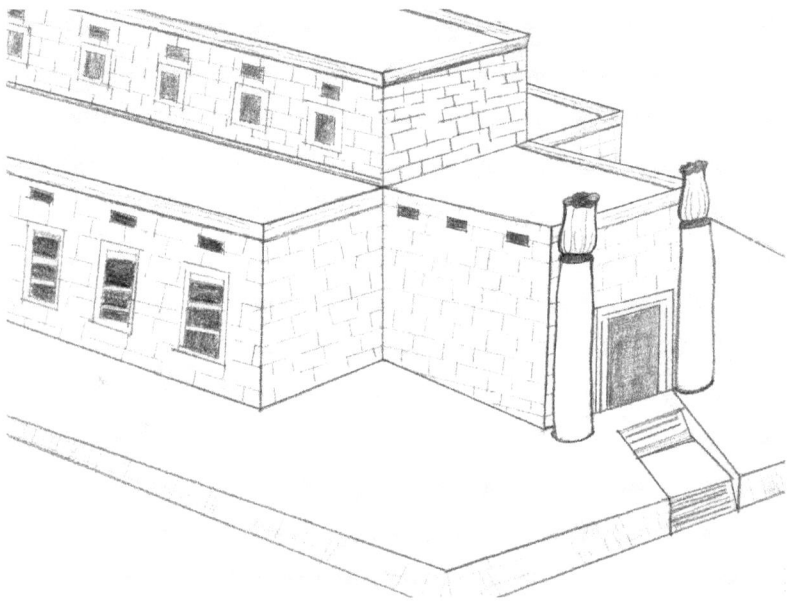

MASHIACH

(Messiah, "Anointed One")
You will cleanse the unholy* and build for Your glory
A physical temple on the former threshing floor.
You will scatter the wicked by Your forceful breath
And establish Your people as priests raised from death!
Prayers will ascend from the Temple Mount,
Inviting Mashiach as a cleansing Fount!
The One whom they pierced will return at their call –

"Baruch haba b'Shem Adonai" – †
Messiah of all!

October 11, 2012

---

* Israel has sovereignty over the Temple Mount, but the Muslim Waqf has custody of the site, formerly home to the first and second Temple. The Al Aqsa Mosque and the Dome of the Rock are "unholy" shrines to Allah, a false god. Due to the security situation, Jews are not allowed to pray on the Temple Mount, even though doing so is legal.

† "Blessed is He who comes in the name of the Lord." Matthew 23:39. Jesus said the Jewish leaders would not see his face again until they spoke these words (quoting Psalm 118:26), in effect inviting Him back as their Messiah!

Time Is Short

In late December, the shortest day of the year,
Is begging the question, "Is His coming near?"
"Time is short, get your house in order.
Don't live for pleasure and feasting! Don't loiter!"
The Spirit is speaking; tune your heart to hear.
Pray for others that have no fear.
It's always the darkest just before the dawn.
Keep your heart expectant; for His appearing you should long.
The Bible says in its very last book,
That Jesus is coming as a thief – we should look!
Revelation sixteen, the words are in red.
The fifteenth verse, this is what He said:
"Blessed is he who watches," Jesus warns.
His words are spoken in the midst of the storm.
God's wrath at a climax, the last bowl poured out,
Earthquake unequaled, cities fall flat!
Hailstones cause blasphemy of perishing men.
Babylon falls, then rejoicing begins!
Heaven is opened, on a white horse He comes,
King of Kings, Lord of Lords, the victory is won!
The devil is bound for a thousand years,
And we who were watching reign with Jesus, no fears!
The story gets better as the Bible ends,
But make sure you're watching and waiting for Him!
His coming as a thief is an obvious clue:
Make yourself ready. He'll tell you what to do.
Jesus, the Bridegroom, wants a bride clothed in white.
Scripture says good deeds are her garments, shining bright.
So let this day, the shortest of the year,
Remind you to start now, get ready right here!

December 21, 2013

Heaven's All Astir

(A Christmas Musical)
Performed by children at Golden Triangle Trinity Church,
Columbus, Mississippi, in 1994.
A play about the birth of Christ viewed from the angels'
perspective in heaven.
Denise Collins: script writer, director, and choreographer
Nancy Petrey: six original songs, music and words

HEAVEN'S ALL ASTIR

(Title Song)

[Scene: Chaotic choir practice]

Joy to the world! Hark! the Herald Angels Sing!
The First Noel the angels did say … Silent Night, Holy Night!
Angels practicing their runs and trills.
Jingle bells, jingle bells, jingle all the way.

(Chorus): Heaven's all astir! Heaven's all astir!
Whirring and flapping! Chorusing and clapping!
Heaven's all astir! Heaven's all astir!
Glad tidings ring! All the angels sing!

Joy surrounds! Happiness abounds!
Angels in the air! Glory everywhere!
Gloria----! Gloria----! (Chorus)

Joy to the world! Wings are unfurled!
He is coming! He is coming! He is coming! He is coming!
Gloria----! Gloria----!
[Congregation sings *Joy to the World*]

October 28, 1994

The Jericho Stomp

(Knowing big things were afoot in heaven, two little angels reminisced about the time when the angels stomped on the walls of Jericho and made the walls fall down. Song has a boogie beat.)

The Jericho Stomp! You could hear it for miles around.
The Jericho Stomp! Michael went out on the town.
The Jericho Stomp! It made a mighty sound.
The Jericho Stomp! It made the walls fall down!

Joshua said, "The battle plans
have come from the Heavenly Chief."
He said, "You just walk it, don't you dare talk it.
Take My ark around the town,
only the trumpets will sound.
A day at a time, six days in all,
Seven times on the seventh day."
The angels all poised, waitin' for the noise,
Came the shout! And they began to sway!

The Jericho Stomp! You could hear it for miles around.
The Jericho Stomp! Michael went out on the town.
The Jericho Stomp! It made a mighty sound.
The Jericho Stomp! It made the walls fall down!

October 28, 1994

HEAVEN'S ABLAZE

(Little angels waltzing vigorously and singing)

Heaven's ablaze with His glorious birth!
Heaven's aglow with a wonderful mirth!
Angels are twirling and cavorting in space!
Shining in the brightness of the smile on God's face!

(Chorus): Hallelujah! Hallelujah! Hallelu—jah!
Hallelujah! Hallelujah! Hallelu—jah!
Hallelujah! Hallelujah! Hallelu—jah!
Hallelujah! I'm praisin' the Lord!

Jesus, our Savior, came into this world –
Glory from heaven in Mary unfurled!
He made His entrance in God's plan of grace,
Shining in the brightness of the smile on God's Face!
(Chorus)

Joseph had dreamed of an angel in bed –
"Name the wee baby 'Yeshua,'" he said.
"He'll save His people, their sins He'll erase,"
Shining in the brightness of the smile on God's face!
(Chorus)

October 28, 1994; verses 2 & 3 – January 31, 2015

HARP SONG

(Little angel is petulant, having been reprimanded for singing off-key.
Choir of small angels joins in the dance.)

I hung my harp on the willow tree 'cause I can't sing.
I hung my harp on the willow tree and folded my wings.
The angels say that my notes are sour and off key.
I'm just too little to play and sing and dance for Thee.
(Spoken slowly) God, do You agree? --
(Pause) And God said:

"Take your harp off the willow tree and play for Me,
Take your harp off the willow tree and dance for Me.
A shoot sprang up from the stump of Jesse, can't you sing?
A root grew out of the dry ground, won't you dance with Me?

David played his harp for Me and sang to Me.
David brought the ark home, and he danced for Me.
Come now and play for the Son of David at His birth.
Sing and dance 'cause the Father sent His Son to earth!"

(Little angel with resolve): I will take the harp,
And I will sing and dance,
And I will make a joyful noise! (off key)

October 20, 1994

73

THE SAVIOR'S LOOKING UP AT ME

(Two little angels looking down from the portals of heaven
at the Baby lying in a manger)

The Savior's looking up at me,
I ask myself, how can it be
That God Almighty sent His Son to earth
a baby boy?
As I look down into His face,
I see His glory and His grace.
How can this Lowly One be bringing
so much joy to me?

The angels applaud His marvelous majesty.
The fingers so tiny once formed you and me.
The feet that once stood beside the throne of God
Are lying in a manger in a cattle stall!

The Savior's looking up at me,
I ask myself, how can it be
That God Almighty sent His Son to earth
a baby boy?
As I look down into His face,
I see His glory and His grace.
How can this Lowly One be bringing
so much joy to me?

October 26, 1994

The Wedding Feast

(You Are Aged Wine)

~ Song based on John 2:1-11 ~

Have you ever heard the story of the wedding in Cana of Galilee?
Have you thought much about the stone pots that were used for the wine?
They were sitting there waiting to be used; they had great capacity,
But till Jesus came they were empty as they could be.
There was a wedding, and Jesus had them filled to the brim with water.
He said, "Draw some out. Take it to the master of the feast."
When the master of the feast tasted the water that was made into wine,
He called the Bridegroom and said, "What you have done is so very fine."
The world serves their best wine at the first and saves the worst till last,
But Jesus has a better idea: He ages His wine.
And as the days grow long, and you don't feel so strong, He will come to you,
Fill you up with Living Water, and He'll change you into finest wine.

CHORUS 1:
You are aged wine. I've been saving you a long time.
You are aged wine. You are a wonder and a sign.
You are aged wine. To everything there is a season and a time.
The Bridegroom has had a long fast. He's saved the very best till last!

You were that water pot that was empty till Jesus came your way.
At the wedding of your spirit, you were filled with Living Water,
just a pot of clay.
Now He'll pour you out, and you'll quench the thirst of a dying world.
He's saved the best till last. You're the finest wine that He has!

CHORUS 2:
You are aged wine. I've been saving you until the end of time.
You are aged wine. You are a wonder and a sign.
You are aged wine. The King is coming soon,
He'll say, "You are Mine."
The Bridegroom at last will have His bride,
and He'll take you to His side.
He'll take you up into the air – for this day you must prepare –
To His throne in New Jerusalem for the wedding feast of the Lamb!

Words & Music by Nancy Petrey, June 12, 1995, © October 23, 1995; revised September 13, 2009

Nancy Petrey pursues her calling to be a Mizpah for Israel by loving Israel and the Jewish people, teaching the church about her Jewish roots, traveling to Israel, holding community Bible studies & prayer meetings, and hosting Passover Seders & speakers from Israel and elsewhere. She has a Master's Degree in Religious Education in the Middle East. Much of her ministry has been in partnership with Janice Bell, a Messianic Jew. Nancy is a church pianist and lives in Petrey, Alabama, with her husband Curtis, who is a retired pastor. They have four children and thirteen grandchildren.

Habitation of Honey is her second book. One more book, *Why Christians Should Care about Their Jewish Roots* is expected this year.

You can follow Nancy's activities in ministry on her blog at www.jewishrootsjourney.blogspot.com or her Facebook page, Mizpah Tikvah Ministries.

ALSO BY NANCY PETREY

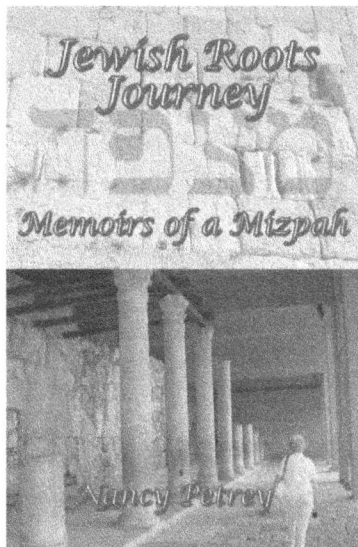

The Appendix section alone ... will make this book a treasure in your home.

Roy & Mary Kendall
Directors
School of Worship in Jerusalem

COMING IN 2015

NANCY PETREY

WHY CHRISTIANS SHOULD CARE
ABOUT THEIR
JEWISH ROOTS

Topical
Line
Drives

Volume 17

More from Energion Publications

Personal Study

Finding My Way in Christianity	Herold Weiss	$16.99
The Jesus Paradigm	David Alan Black	$17.99
When People Speak for God	Henry Neufeld	$17.99

Christian Living

Faith in the Public Square	Robert D. Cornwall	$16.99
Grief: Finding the Candle of Light	Jody Neufeld	$8.99
Crossing the Street	Robert LaRochelle	$16.99

Bible Study

Learning and Living Scripture	Lentz/Neufeld	$12.99
From Inspiration to Understanding	Edward W. H. Vick	$24.99
Luke: A Participatory Study Guide	Geoffrey Lentz	$8.99
Philippians: A Participatory Study Guide	Bruce Epperly	$9.99
Ephesians: A Participatory Study Guide	Robert D. Cornwall	$9.99
Evidence for the Bible	Elgin Hushbeck, Jr.	

Theology

Creation in Scripture	Herold Weiss	$12.99
Creation: the Christian Doctrine	Edward W. H. Vick	$12.99
Ultimate Allegiance	Robert D. Cornwall	$9.99
History and Christian Faith	Edward W. H. Vick	$9.99
The Church Under the Cross	William Powell Tuck	$11.99
The Journey to the Undiscovered Country	William Powell Tuck	$9.99
Eschatology: A Participatory Study Guide	Edward W. H. Vick	$9.99
Philosophy for Believers	Edward W. H. Vick	$14.99
Christianity and Secularism	Elgin Hushbeck, Jr.	$16.99

Ministry

Operation Olive Branch	Hannah May	$16.99
Clergy Table Talk	Kent Ira Groff	$9.99
So Much Older Then …	Robert LaRochelle	$9.99

Generous Quantity Discounts Available
Dealer Inquiries Welcome
Energion Publications — P.O. Box 841
Gonzalez, FL 32560
Website: http://energionpubs.com
Phone: (850) 525-3916

www.ingramcontent.com/pod-product-compliance
Lightning Source LLC
LaVergne TN
LVHW041234080426
835508LV00011B/1199